NATO Aircraft in colour

Robbie Shaw

Copyright © Jane's Publishing Company Limited 1986

First published in the United Kingdom in 1986 by
Jane's Publishing Company Limited
238 City Road, London EC1V 2PU

ISBN 0 7106 0399 1

Printed in the United Kingdom by
Netherwood Dalton & Co Ltd, Huddersfield

JANE'S

Cover illustrations

Front: A General Dynamics F-16A operated by 323 Sqn of the Royal
Netherlands Air Force rotates for lift-off. It is armed with a pair of
wingtip-mounted Sidewinder dogfight missiles and carries a 250
Imp gal centreline drop tank.

Back: Mirage F.1C of the 30th Fighter Wing of the French Air
Force cleans up after taking off from RAF Binbrook. A single air-to-
air missile training round is carried on the starboard wingtip.

Right: A-10A 80-0194/WR of the USAF's 509th Tactical Fighter
Squadron, 81st Tactical Fighter Wing, taxies clear of the runway
after landing at its home base, RAF Bentwaters. The 81st is the
largest wing in the USAF, comprising six squadrons of A-10
Thunderbolt IIs based at Bentwaters and Woodbridge. The wing
maintains detachments at the four forward operating locations
(FOLs) at Sembach, Leipheim, Norvenich and Ahlhorn in West
Germany; the latter three bases are Luftwaffe airfields. The USAF
regularly rehearses its European reinforcement role, deploying
squadrons of A-10s and other types across the Atlantic to European
bases, where they operate for two to four weeks before returning
home.

For Eileen

Introduction

In a book of this size it is not possible to cover every type operated by the air arms of NATO. I have therefore tried to represent the most common and well known aircraft, in particular those flown by more than one service.

I have been an avid aircraft enthusiast ever since I was taken to my first air display at RNAS Abbotsinch at the age of twelve. Now serving as an air traffic controller in the Royal Air Force, and with my camera always at my side, I am in the fortunate position of being able to photograph aircraft every working day — and on a large number of rest days besides.

I have always enjoyed flying, and to date have logged over 500 passenger hours in 69 different types, including two of my three favourites, the F-4 Phantom and F-101 Voodoo. (A flight in a Lightning still eludes me.) Indeed, I have managed to get into the air so readily that it was only a matter of time before I tried my hand at air-to-air photography. This I now regard as the ultimate test of ability for an aviation photographer, particularly when one is encased in a helmet, oxygen mask, g-suit and immersion suit and strapped tightly to an ejection seat in the narrow confines of a fast-jet cockpit.

All of the photographs in this book were taken with Pentax cameras. I have two ME Super bodies and use Pentax 50mm, 40-80mm zoom, 135mm and 200mm lenses plus a Hoya 400mm lens, all fitted with UV filter. Shutter speeds vary from about 10sec for night shots to 1/500sec for fast-moving jets. Air-to-air shots are generally taken at 1/250sec. Except for the picture on page 9, which was taken on Fuji, I used Kodachrome 64 film.

I am indebted to many people for their assistance. In particular I wish to thank 233 OCU, 74 Sqn, 79 Sqn and 360 Sqn RAF, Strategic Air Command USAF, Air Command of the Canadian Armed Forces, and the Spanish and Turkish air forces.

ROBBIE SHAW
June 1986

Left: Boeing E-3A Sentry LX-N90447 lines up on the runway at RAF Fairford. A total of 18 of these aircraft are operated by the NATO Airborne Early Warning Force (AEWF) from Geilenkirchen in West Germany, with permanent detachments as far afield as Oerland in Norway and Konya in Turkey. The AEWF is a truly multinational organisation: the aircraft belong to the alliance rather than to individual countries, while the crews are drawn from every NATO air force except the RAF. It is thus not unusual to find Greek and Turkish radar operators working contentedly side by side – something their respective countries have failed to do.

Above: Three NATO countries – Britain, West Germany and Italy – build and operate the Panavia Tornado. They have set up a joint aircrew training organisation – the Trinational Tornado Training Establishment (TTTE) – at RAF Cottesmore. Epitomising the NATO spirit of co-operation is Tornado MM7005/I-91: an Italian Air Force aircraft flown by a German student under the supervision of a British instructor.

The mainstay of the US naval strike/attack force is the Grumman A-6E Intruder. One squadron of Intruders, plus four KA-6D tankers, is deployed aboard each US Navy aircraft carrier. A-6E 157013A/J507 of VA-35 was photographed aboard the nuclear-powered USS *Nimitz*. Spotted on the deck behind it are two EA-6B Prowlers from VAQ-135. The Prowler is a four-crew Intruder variant used for electronic countermeasures. **Operated by:** USN, USMC

Photographed during a squadron exchange at RAF Coltishall is Greek Air Force A-7H Corsair II 159943, normally based at Larissa. Based on the larger F-8 Crusader, the A-7 is a single-seat carrier-based light attack aircraft powered by the Allison TF41 turbofan, a licence-built non-afterburning version of the Rolls-Royce Spey. The USAF A-7D entered service in 1968, and both Navy and Air Force aircraft saw combat in South-east Asia. The Corsair II has now been superseded in Tactical Air Command by the A-10, and all USAF A-7s serve in the Air Force Reserve and Air National Guard. **Operated by:** Greek AF, Portuguese AF, USAF, USN

5

In January 1973 the Fairchild A-10A Thunder-bolt II won the competition to become the USAF's new close support aircraft, beating the Northrop A-9. Operating in conjunction with Army AH-1S Cobra helicopters, the A-10A is a lethal tankbuster. Its GAU-8 Avenger seven-barrel 30mm cannon can fire no fewer than 4,200 rounds per minute, and its 11 stores pylons have a total capacity of 16,000lb. Like all US combat aircraft, the A-10A is capable of being refuelled in flight. A-10A 81-0944/WR of the 510th Tactical Fighter Squadron, 81st Tactical Fighter Wing, is shown on the approach to its base at RAF Bentwaters, carrying an ECM pod on the port outboard pylon. **Operated by:** USAF

The design of the B-52 Stratofortress makes it very susceptible to crosswinds, as can be seen in this shot of a B-52G landing at RAF Fairford. This aircraft, 80207, is from the 69th Bombardment Squadron, 42nd Bombardment Wing, based at Loring AFB, Maine. Though Strategic Air Command B-52s stand alert loaded with free-fall nuclear bombs or Air Launched Cruise Missiles (ALCMs), their cavernous bomb bays can also carry great weights of conventional bombs and anti-shipping mines. Only the B-52G and H remain in service, a large number of Ds having been scrapped recently as a strategic arms limitation measure. **Operated by:** USAF

7

Above: Buccaneer S2B XZ430 of 208 Sqn pictured at RAF Honington shortly before the unit moved to its new home at Lossiemouth. Along with 12 Sqn, No 208 forms the RAF's maritime strike force, armed with Martel and Sea Eagle missiles. The Buccaneer is about to receive an avionics update which will allow it to remain in front-line service well into the 1990s. Although subsonic, this robust aircraft has proved during USAF "Red Flag" exercises that it could survive and perform well over a modern battlefield. The "Bucc" possesses a unique rotating bomb bay door which can also be used to carry additional fuel. **Operated by:** RAF

Right: Immediately identifiable by its unusual shape, the Saab 35 Draken is operated in the attack role by 725 Eskadron of the Royal Danish Air Force and for reconnaissance by 729 Eskadron, both based at Karup. Saab 35XD AR-117 of the latter unit is shown landing at RAF Waddington in October 1985. Note the camera port on the underside of the nose of the aircraft. **Operated by:** Royal Danish AF

Above: The McDonnell Douglas F-4 Phantom II has for the past two decades been the backbone of many NATO air arms. The West's most successful post-war combat aircraft, with over 5,000 built since it flew for the first time in 1958, the Phantom will almost certainly still be in service at the beginning of the 21st century. Some countries are planning avionics updates, while the USAF has introduced a new one-piece canopy to reduce vulnerability to birdstrikes. The Phantom has been in combat with US forces in South-east Asia, the Israel Defence Force in the Middle East, and currently with the Islamic Iranian Air Force in the war with Iraq. With reheat engaged, Luftwaffe F-4F 37 + 93 of Jagdbombergeschwader 36 roars down the runway at Bruggen before taking off to return to its base at Hopsten.

Right: F-4J ZE352/G of 74 "Tiger" Sqn RAF returning over a snowbound East Anglia to its Wattisham base after a low-level training sortie in Wales. Fifteen former USMC F-4Js were taken on charge by 74 Sqn in 1984 to cover the gap in the UK air defences caused by the move of 23 Sqn to the Falkland Islands.

Left: F-4E 70302 of the Turkish Air Force seen just after take-off from its base at Eskisehir in November 1985. Turkey operates two squadrons of F-4Es and a single squadron of RF-4Es from Eskisehir, and a further three squadrons of F-4Es from Erhac. **Operated by:** Federal German AF, Greek AF, Spanish AF, Turkish AF, RAF, USAF, USN, USMC

Below: The Northrop F-5A lightweight tactical fighter first flew in 1959. With its modest price tag and respectable performance, this uncomplicated little aircraft soon began to accumulate export orders. Canadair built the F5A/B under licence for the Canadian and Netherlands air forces, while CASA did likewise for the Spanish Air Force. The latest version, the F-5E/F Tiger II, is still in production and serving with many Third World countries. But the introduction of the F-16 and F-18 means that the numbers of F-5s with NATO air forces are now dwindling. The Norwegian Air Force, for instance, has reduced its F-5 force from five squadrons to one, though many of the surplus aircraft have been passed on to the Turkish Air Force. F-5E 01560 of the USAF's 527th Aggressor Squadron lands at its base, RAF Alconbury. The USAF uses the F-5E solely for dissimilar air combat training.

Left: The Spanish Air Force operates the licence-built SF-5A, SRF-5A and SF-5B. One of the latter, AE9-033/732-33, is seen here performing a barrel roll in the course of a training flight from its base at Talavera la Real in western Spain in December 1985. Talavera is home to 731 and 732 Escuadrones, which form the Escuela de Reactores, the Spanish equivalent of an RAF tactical weapons unit.

Above: All the Canadian AF CF-5As are fitted with bolt-on probes, making them the only F-5s in NATO capable of in-flight refuelling. 116705 is seen here topping up from a CAF CC-137. This aircraft belongs to 419 Sqn, operating from Cold Lake, Alberta, as the CAF's fast-jet operational training unit. In-flight refuelling is a requirement of the OTU course, as the operational CF-5 units, 433 and 434 Sqns, would in times of tension deploy across the Atlantic to protect NATO's northern flank. **Operated by:** CAF, Greek AF, Royal Netherlands AF, Royal Norwegian AF, Spanish AF, Turkish AF, USAF and USN

Above: At rest on board USS *John F. Kennedy* is F-14A Tomcat 161163/AC106 of VF-11. Each carrier air wing has two squadrons of Tomcats tasked with fleet air defence and provision of top cover for the carrierborne strike force. Armed with Phoenix, Sparrow and Sidewinder missiles and a single Vulcan cannon, the Tomcat is the world's most powerful naval fighter. **Operated by:** USN

Right: Bearing a resemblance to the F-14, though lacking its variable geometry, the McDonnell Douglas F-15 Eagle is also optimised for the air superiority role, equipped with a lightweight, long-range pulse-Doppler radar, Sidewinder and Sparrow air-to-air mis-siles and a single 20mm cannon. The next variant off the production line will be the F-15E Strike Eagle, designed to supplant the F-111 in the nuclear strike role. Shown taking off from Tyndall AFB, Florida, are F-15As 60104 and 60113 of the 48th Fighter Inter-ceptor Squadron, based at Langley AFB, Virginia. **Operated by:** USAF

After an 11-month fly-off the USAF selected the General Dynamics F-16 in preference to the Northrop YF-17 as its new lightweight fighter, planning to procure a total of 1,388 aircraft. Shortly afterwards Belgium, Denmark, the Netherlands and Norway preferred the F-16 to the Mirage F.1 as a replacement for their ageing F-104 Starfighters. There is no doubt that the Fighting Falcon, as the F-16 is known, is a superb aircraft, though its cost is significantly higher than anticipated. It is also extremely versatile, being used for strike/attack, reconnaissance and air defence. Illustrated is F-16A E-198 of 723 Eskadron Royal Danish Air Force, seen departing RAF Waddington en route to its home base at Aalborg.

J270, an F-16B of 323 Sqn Royal Netherlands Air Force, leads an F-16A of 322 Sqn during a training sortie. Both units operate from Leeu-warden in the air defence role. These aircraft are preparing to carry out a rendezvous with a USAF KC-135 tanker in Danish airspace: note the open refuelling receptacle on the spine aft of the cockpit.

Left: Royal Netherlands Air Force F-16 approaches the refuelling boom of a USAF KC-135 tanker. Note the cannon port below the cockpit of the fighter. **Operated by:** Belgian AF, Royal Danish AF, Royal Netherlands AF, Royal Norwegian AF and USAF

Right: After delays caused by problems with its tail structure, deliveries of the F-18 Hornet to the US Navy and Marines and Canadian Armed Forces have resumed, and Navy and Marine squadrons have completed operational tours at sea. Here CF-18A 188710 of the CAF's 410 Sqn, based at CFB Cold Lake, taxies past a CAF Dakota at Shearwater, Nova Scotia. To keep costs down CAF aircraft retain the folding wings, strengthened landing gear and arrester hook of USN and USMC aircraft. This year the Spanish Air Force will take delivery of its first Hornets, using them to replace F-4C Phantoms and Mirage IIIs.

CF-18A 188723 seen at Cold Lake soon after delivery. Still to be assigned to a squadron, the aircraft carries the markings of the base engineering wing. Canadian Hornets operate in both the attack and air defence roles, replacing the CF-101 Voodoo and CF-104 Starfighter. 410 Sqn is the CF-18 training unit, with 425 Sqn at Bagotville providing air defence. 409, 421 and 439 Sqns, based at Baden Soellingen in West Germany, comprise No 1 Canadian Air Group. **Operated by:** CAF, Spanish AF, USN and USMC

There are only two airworthy McDonnell F-101 Voodoos left, both operated by 414 "Black Knights" Sqn CAF from North Bay, Ontario. One is a CF-101F, fitted with dual flight controls, the other is the solitary EF-101B "Electric Jet". This ex-US National Guard aircraft, sporting a unique gloss-black paint scheme, is used for ECM training. Seen here taking off from CFB Chatham, New Brunswick, the aircraft has a natural metal nose as a result of a repair following a nose-wheel collapse on landing. **Operated by:** CAF

23

Above: The contribution of Lockheed's F-104 Starfighter to NATO cannot be overstated. Along with the Phantom, Starfighters made up a large proportion of the alliance's combat aircraft in the 1960s and 1970s. This controversial "missile with a man in it" came in for a lot of criticism because of the large number of accidents it suffered, particularly in German service. But the loss rate based on flying time and numbers of aircraft proved to be no worse than those of comparable aircraft such as the Lightning. Although the West German Luftwaffe and Marineflieger lost over 200 Starfighters, it should be remembered that they had over 900 aircraft to start with. F-104S MM6705/5-43 of the Italian Air Force departs RAF Fairford after the 1985 International Air Tattoo, bound for its home base at Rimini.

Right: The German switch from Starfighter to Tornado is nearly complete, with only one F-104 wing remaining in service. F-104G 26 + 74 of Marinefliegergeschwader 2, based at Eggebeck, taxies to the ramp at RAF Alconbury. **Operated by:** Federal German Air Force, Federal German Navy, Greek AF, Italian AF and Turkish AF

Convair's F-106 Delta Dart all-weather interceptor, developed from its predecessor the F-102 Delta Dagger, is now in the twilight of its career. It is now being superseded in the air defence role by the F-4 and F-15, and only five squadrons – four of them Air National Guard units – remain operational. Pictured here are F-106As of the 194th Fighter Interceptor Squadron, California ANG, and 186th Fighter Interceptor Squadron, Montana ANG, on the ramp at Tyndall AFB, Florida. The 194th FIS has since exchanged its F-106s for F-4D Phantoms. **Operated by:** USAF

The General Dynamics F-111 tactical fighter was the first swing-wing aircraft to enter service. Designed as a long-range tactical fighter-bomber for the USAF and as a carrier-borne strike aircraft, the F-111 failed to live up to expectations in the latter role and was dropped by the US Navy. Fifty F-111Ks were ordered for the RAF but the contract was cancelled in the defence cuts of 1968. The F-111 currently equips four USAF tactical fighter wings, with the FB-111 strategic bomber version being operated by a further two. An F-111F of the 493rd Tactical Fighter Squadron, 48th Tactical Fighter Wing, based at RAF Lakenheath, is seen on departure from RAF Alconbury. **Operated by:** USAF

Although the Harrier entered service in 1969 it was not until the aircraft acquitted itself superbly in the Falklands War that scepticism about the value of V/STOL operations was finally dispelled. The US Marine Corps took little persuading, however, and ordered its first Harriers, designated AV-8, in 1969. Today the McDonnell Douglas/BAe AV-8B, with a more powerful engine and larger wing and weapon load, is in service with the Marines, while the RAF is soon to receive its British counterpart, the Harrier GR5. Pictured here is Harrier GR3 XZ131/N of 233 Operational Conversion Unit, seen near its Wittering base in December 1985. **Operated by:** Spanish Navy, RAF and USMC

Developed from the Harrier, the Sea Harrier FRS1 is operated by 800 and 801 Naval Air Squadrons for deployment aboard the carriers *Ark Royal*, *Illustrious* and *Invincible*. No 899 Sqn at Yeovilton is the training unit. Major external differences from its land-based counter-part are the raised cockpit and Ferranti Blue Fox radar in a nose which folds to port for easier stowage on carriers. Not a single Sea Harrier was lost in air-to-air combat in the Falklands War, and the type was dubbed "La Muerta Negra" (Black Death) by Argentinian pilots. The winged fist on the fin of ZD579/710, seen landing at Duxford in September 1985, identifies it as belonging to 899 Sqn. **Operated by:** RN

29

Above: The Jaguar is built jointly by British Aerospace and Aérospatiale of France. Initially five versions were planned — single and two-seaters for both the British and French air forces, and a single-seater for use from French Navy aircraft carriers — but the last was abandoned in favour of the Super Etendard. In French Air Force service the two-seater trainer is known as the Jaguar E and the single-seater as the Jaguar A. French Jaguars have been involved in the fight against insurgents in the African state of Chad and some have been lost to ground fire. This Jaguar E, E22/11-ME of the Toul-based EC2/11, is seen landing at RAF Bruggen.

Right: RAF Jaguars differ externally from their French counterparts, having a chisel nose containing a laser rangefinder, and a fin-mounted radar warning receiver. The British aircraft also have an advanced inertial navigation and weapon-aiming system. RAF Germany's Jaguars have been replaced in the strike role by the Tornado, but one reconnaissance squadron remains in service, its aircraft carrying cameras and infra-red linescan in a large centreline pod. Jaguar GR1 XZ362/27 of No 2 Sqn from Laarbruch, one of the reconnaissance units, is seen on take-off from RAF Brawdy. **Operated by:** French AF and RAF

Below: The Lightning was for many years the mainstay of the RAF air-defence force, at one time equipping nine squadrons. Many people remember with awe the Lightning's air show speciality, the noisy vertical climb in full reheat. On one occasion recently an F-16 did something similar, prompting a watching USAF officer to remark to an RAF colleague: "That F-16 can climb as good as any Lightning." To which the RAF man replied: "But could it do it twenty years ago?" Today the Lightning survives only with the Lightning Training Flight and Nos 5 and 11 Sqns at RAF Binbrook. Here Lightning F6 XR754/AE of 5 Sqn bares its shark's teeth.

Right: Evident in this view of Lightning F6 XR753/AC of 5 Sqn on the approach to RAF Binbrook are the characteristic wing leading-edge camber, refuelling probe, twin Aden 30mm cannon in the ventral tank and single missile on each nose pylon. **Operated by:** RAF

Left: The Fiat (Aeritalia) G.91 was the winner of a NATO competition to produce a lightweight attack aircraft. In the event the type, in G.91R single-seater and G.91T two-seat trainer form, was procured only by the German, Italian and Portuguese air forces. Later a twin-engined variant, the G.91Y, was built for the Italian AF. Apart from a few target-towing aircraft, the Luftwaffe has replaced its G.91s with the Alpha Jet, passing on some G.91s to

top up the Portuguese fleet. This G.91R3 of 301 Escuadron of the Portuguese Air Force, based at Montijo, south-west of Lisbon, is seen here outside a hardened shelter at Kleine Brogel in Belgium. **Operated by:** Federal German AF, Italian AF and Portuguese AF

Above: The Mirage III, the first of Dassault's highly successful family of delta-winged combat aircraft, was designed initially as a Mach 2

high-altitude all-weather interceptor. Reconnaissance, fighter-bomber and two-seat training versions were subsequently developed. The Mirage III is now being replaced in French Air Force service by the Mirage F.1 and Mirage 2000. Seen here lining up to take off from RAF Wildenrath is Mirage IIIE 13-QH of the Armée de l'Air's EC1/13, based at Colmar. **Operated by:** French AF and Spanish AF

Left: The Mirage IVA long-range nuclear bomber is the largest of the Mirage family and forms a major part of the French nuclear deterrent. A total of 18 Mirage IVAs are currently being overhauled and upgraded to IVP standard to prolong their service lives into the 1990s. The deterrent fleet is dispersed amongst a number of bases, with no more than four aircraft at any one location. This Mirage IVA is carrying out a spectacular rocket-assisted take-off from Creil in northern France. **Operated by:** French AF

Right: The Mirage 5, a simpler version of the Mirage III, is optimised for ground attack. Using the same airframe and engine as the Mirage 3, but with much simplified avionics and a correspondingly increased fuel capacity, it retains the Mach 2 capability of the Mirage III. It also requires less maintenance than the III and is able to operate from semi-prepared airfields. Photographed on take-off from RAF Wyton is BR 03 a reconnaissance Mirage 5BR of 42 Sqn of the Belgian AF, based at Florennes. **Operated by:** Belgian AF, French AF

Left: The Mirage F.1 entered French AF service in 1973. Built in four versions, it has sold extremely well. The F.1B two-seat trainer, F.1C interceptor and F.1CR reconnaissance variants are in current French service, later examples of the F.1C being fitted with an in-flight refuelling probe. The ground attack F.1E is operated by the Spanish AF alongside its F.1Cs. Seen taxiing in at RAF Binbrook is F.1C 30-SG from EC30, based at Reims. It is carrying a 1,200lit fuel tank on the centreline pylon, and is fitted with wingtip rails for Sidewinder or Matra Magic air-to-air missiles. **Operated by:** French AF, Greek AF, Spanish AF

Above: The Mirage 2000C is now in service with the French AF, equipping EC2 at Dijon. In the air defence role it is powered by a SNECMA M53 turbofan engine; armament includes two DEFA 30mm cannon, with up to nine attachments for external stores. Also in squadron service is the 2000B tandem two-seat trainer. Photographed in a two-tone air-superiority paint scheme at Aalborg in Denmark is 2000C 2-EL of EC1/2. **Operated by:** French AF

39

On completion of training at the Tri-National Tornado Training Establishment, RAF crews go to the Tactical Weapons Conversion Unit at Honington. GR1 strike/attack Tornadoes also operate from Marham (27 and 617 Sqns), Bruggen (9, 14, 17 and 31 Sqns) and Laarbruch (15, 16 and 20 Sqns). With its two-man crew and terrain-following radar, the Tornado is an ideal low-level strike aircraft. It can be armed with a large variety of weapons, including the JP233 runway denial system and nuclear, conventional and laser-guided bombs. German Tornadoes can carry the very effective MW-1 anti-tank weapon, and also practice buddy-buddy air refuelling. Tornado GR1 ZA373 of the TWCU demonstrates its all-weather capability by taking off from Honington in a torrential downpour. **Operated by:** Federal German AF, Federal German Navy, Italian AF, RAF

The Tornado F2 Air Defence Version is operated within NATO only by the RAF, with which it will replace the Lightning and some Phantoms. The F2, with its lengthened nose to accommodate the Foxhunter radar, looks much sleeker than its "mud-moving" counterpart. All F2s are painted in air-superiority grey and armed with Sidewinder and Sky Flash missiles. Tornado F2 ZD934/AD of 229 Operational Conversion Unit is shown going through its paces at an air show at Duxford. 229 OCU is based at Coningsby, home also of the Phantom OCU, No 228. **Operated by:** RAF

The Atlantic twin-turboprop anti-submarine aircraft has been in service for over 20 years, during which its effectiveness has been called into question a number of times. The Royal Netherlands Navy certainly had its share of problems with the type, and has now replaced it with the P-3C Orion. The West German Navy is also looking into the possibility of replacing the Atlantics operated by Marine-fliegergeschwader 3. This unit operates four aircraft converted for the electronic intelligence (ELINT) role. Aérospatiale is currently producing the updated Atlantic ANG, ordered by the French Navy. Italian Air Force Atlantic MM40111/41-73 of 41 Stormo, based at Fontanarossa, is seen here landing at Greenham Common. Italian Atlantics are operated by the Air Force but have mixed Air Force/Navy crews. **Operated by:** French Navy, Federal German Navy, Italian AF

When the Canadian Defence Ministry decided on a replacement for the CP-107 Argus maritime patrol aircraft the choice fell on a combination of the airframe, powerplant and basic aircraft systems of the Lockheed P-3 Orion with the electronics and data-processing equipment of the Lockheed S-3 Viking carrier-based anti-submarine aircraft. The result, designated CP-140 Aurora, is more capable than USN Orions. A total of 18 aircraft were bought to equip four squadrons. Seen here taxiing out at Greenham Common is 140110 of the Greenwood Wing. **Operated by:** CAF

Left: The Canberra T17s operated by 360 Sqn RAF in the ECM training role are kept extremely busy meeting the demands of NATO units. The squadron spends a lot of time away from its Wyton base on exercises right across Alliance territory from Norway to Italy. Even when in transit the T17s are earning their keep: on a leg from Wyton to Gibraltar, say, en route the aircraft would provide jamming for French naval units in the Bay of Biscay and for Portuguese radar or fighters before landing at Gibraltar. The aircraft are currently undergoing a partial avionics update, and it is likely that these converted B2 bombers will be around for a long time to come. WF916/EL was photographed in January 1986 while working with RN ships from Portland. **Operated by:** RAF

Above: Boeing E-3A LX-N90456 of the NATO Airborne Early Warning Force photographed at RAF Waddington, where a detachment of E-3As is in residence. The USAF's E-3 unit, the 552nd Airborne Warning and Control Wing, at Tinker AFB, Oklahoma, has a large fleet of E-3A and E-3C Sentries, a number of which are always deployed around the world to locations such as Keflavik in Iceland, Kadena in Japan and Riyadh in Saudi Arabia. **Operated by:** NATO, USAF

Above: Converted from the General Dynamics F-111A, the EF-111A Raven is the latest addition to NATO's electronic counter-measures (ECM) fleet. The success of offen-sive operations can depend greatly on the attacker's ability to jam radar and communications systems, and this is what the Raven, with its three tons of electronic equipment, does better than any other type in Western service. A total of 42 F-111As are being converted to Raven configuration to equip two squadrons, the 42nd Electronic Countermeasures Squadron (ECS) at RAF Upper Heyford and the 388th ECS at Mountain Home AFB, Idaho. 67-034, operated by the 42nd ECS, was photographed at RAF Fairford in July 1985. **Operated by:** USAF

Right: Nimrod AEW3, Britain's attempt to produce its own advanced airborne early warn-ing system, has had a lengthy and troubled development. At the beginning of 1986 two aircraft were being used at RAF Waddington for trials aimed at bringing radar performance up to an agreed proportion of the specification by mid-year. If this is not achieved, RAF will insist on a foreign solution such as the E-2 Hawkeye or E-3 Sentry. This picture of Nimrod AEW3 XV263 was taken during a flypast at the Farnborough Show. **Operated by:** RAF

Fokker has produced several military versions of its best-selling F.27 Friendship twin-turboprop airliner. These include the Troopship transport, Maritime Enforcer surveillance and anti-submarine aircraft, Sentinel border patrol and standoff reconnaissance version, the proposed Kingbird AEW variant, and (illustrated) the F.27 Maritime unarmed maritime patroller. The aircraft shown here, F.27MP D2-03 of the Spanish Air Force, is used principally for search and rescue, a role in which its 12hr endurance is invaluable. **Operated by:** Royal Netherlands AF, Spanish AF

While the main military application of the Dassault Falcon 20 executive jet is as a VIP transport, two NATO air forces also use the type for ECM training. Though rather short of electrical power for the electronic systems needed in this role, it is very manoeuvrable: Canadian Falcon 20s, designated C-117, have been known to give USAF F-106s a run for their money! EC-117 117505 of 414 Sqn is seen here at its base at North Bay, Ontario. **Operated in the ECM role by:** CAF, Royal Norwegian AF

Left: Known as "The Mighty Hunter" after its Biblical namesake, the Nimrod is unique amongst maritime patrol aircraft in being all jet-powered. Current operational standard for the type is the MR2, with the superb Searchwater radar; certain aircraft have also been fitted with in-flight refuelling probes. In addition to a large bomb bay which can accommodate torpedoes, bombs and mines, the Nimrod has underwing hardpoints for Sidewinder self-defence missiles. Nimrod MR2P XV239 of the Kinloss Wing airs its bomb bay during a display at RAF Wyton. **Operated by:** RAF

Below: First introduced into service in 1962, the Lockheed P-3 Orion anti-submarine aircraft is still in production nearly a quarter of a century later, with the P-3C Update 3 version currently being delivered to the US Navy. This has released older P-3As for conversion to cargo/utility configuration. The USN also operates Orions on electronic intelligence and research duties. With a ten-man crew, the Orion can fly missions of up to 17hr duration. P-3B 601 of 333 Skvadron Royal Norwegian AF, based at Andoya in northern Norway, is seen here on final approach to RAF Greenham Common. **Operated by:** CAF (CP-140 Aurora), Royal Netherlands Navy, Royal Norwegian AF, Portuguese AF, Spanish AF, USN

The problems besetting AEW Nimrod have obliged the antique Shackleton AEW2 to soldier on long past its retirement date. Ground crews have worked miracles to keep the ageing fleet airborne, but a growing shortage of spares means that they will not be able to keep this up for much longer. WL790 is seen taking off from RAF Brawdy. **Operated by:** RAF

Electronic surveillance is NATO's main means of keeping tabs on what is happening along its borders with the Warsaw Pact. In the USAF this task is performed by the Boeing RC-135s of the 343rd Strategic Reconnaissance Squadron (SRS), 55th Strategic Reconnaissance Wing (SRW), based at Offutt AFB, Nebraska. The squadron is kept extremely busy and has aircraft permanently deployed to Alaska, Greece, Japan, and Mildenhall in the UK. Photographed on the approach to Mildenhall is RC-135U 14849. **Operated by:** USAF

Above: Although the Lockheed SR-71 Blackbird is a regular sight around RAF Mildenhall, aviation enthusiasts cannot fail to be impressed every time this phenomenal machine flies. It is hard to believe that this futuristic design, still the world's fastest aircraft, has now been in service with the 1st SRS, 9th SRW, at Beale AFB, California, for over 20 years. Details of the performance of this high-flying reconnaissance aircraft are still classified, but it has held the world records for straight-line and closed-circuit speed since 1976. The 9th SRW has permanent detachments of Blackbirds at Kadena (Okinawa) and Mildenhall. SR-71A 17980 is seen here taking off from the latter base. **Operated by:** USAF

Right: Built at the same Lockheed "Skunk Works" as the Blackbird, the TR-1 high-altitude reconnaissance aircraft is basically an updated U-2. The TR-1 is in production for Strategic Air Command and serves with the 9th SRW at Beale and the 17th RW at RAF Alconbury. Like the SR-71 crews, TR-1 pilots wear a full pressure suit for protection at the extreme altitudes at which operational missions are flown. Down at the lower edge of the envelope, the TR-1's long-span, high-lift wing and delicate undercarriage make landings a tricky business. TR-1A 01078 of the 95th Reconnaissance Squadron, 17th RW, was photographed on take-off from Alconbury. **Operated by:** USAF

Lockheed's C-5 Galaxy, affectionately called "Fat Albert" by its crews, is easily the largest aircraft in the West. A total of 81 of these long-range heavy transport aircraft were delivered to the USAF's Military Airlift Command. As well as hauling outsize cargo, the Galaxy can operate in the paratrooping role, carrying no fewer than 345 fully equipped troops. The C-5B version is now in production, and an initial batch of 50 have been ordered. This C-5A, 00463 of the 436th Military Airlift Wing (MAW), is seen departing Mildenhall at the start of a transatlantic flight to its home base, Dover AFB, Delaware. **Operated by:** USAF

Fat Albert's little brother is the Lockheed C-141 Starlifter. This strategic long-range cargo aircraft was developed to replace the USAF's piston-engined transports, and a total of 284 were taken on charge. Apart from four NC-141A research aircraft, the whole fleet was subsequently converted to C-141B standard, receiving two plugs in the fuselage which increased its length by 23ft 4in, and an in-flight refuelling receptacle. All aircraft are now being resprayed in the European 1 "lizard" colour scheme, displayed here by aircraft 60183 of the 438th MAW, McGuire AFB, New Jersey, on climb-out from RAF Alconbury. **Operated by:** USAF

Below: Old Dakotas never die, they just fade away – very slowly. Over half a century after the type's first flight the C-47 is still in regular service with the Greek and Turkish air forces, and in Canada with 402 Reserve Squadron. The Dakotas operated by the Italian Air Force on calibration duties are now being replaced by the Aeritalia G.222. This IAF C-47, MM61893/14-46 of 8 Gruppo, 14 Stormo, based at Pratica di Mare, is seen landing at RAF Fairford. **Operated by:** CAF, Greek AF, Italian AF, Turkish AF

Right: The Lockheed C-130 Hercules has now been in production for 31 years, and looks set to run on well into the next century. This ubiquitous transport has been built in so many variants for so many countries that there isn't room to list them all here. Illustrated on the approach to RAF Mildenhall is MC-130E 40561 of the 7th Special Operations Squadron, based at Rhein-Main. **Operated by:** Belgian AF, CAF, Royal Danish AF, Greek AF, Italian AF, Royal Norwegian AF, Portuguese AF, Spanish AF, Turkish AF, RAF, USAF, USN, USMC, USCG

Canada and Norway use the Falcon 20 in both the ECM training and VIP transport roles. Norway's 335 Skvadron has one transport Falcon and the CAF's 412 Sqn has three. The US Coast Guard also uses the type for maritime surveillance. Canadian ECM Falcon operator No 414 Sqn, based at North Bay, Ontario, uses one unconverted aircraft, CC-117 117504, as a squadron hack and for type conversion. It is illustrated here during a training flight in October 1985. **Operated by:** Belgian AF, CAF, French AF, Norwegian AF, Portuguese AF, Spanish AF, USCG

The Canadair Challenger is in service with two NATO countries. It is replacing Luftwaffe Hansa Jet and JetStar VIP transports, while in Canada it serves as the CC-144 VIP transport with 412 Sqn and as the EC-144 ECM aircraft will join 414 Sqn in 1987. CC-144 144608 of 412 Sqn was photographed standing by to receive boarders at CFB Uplands near Ottawa. **Operated by:** CAF, Federal German AF

Left: Developed from the successful Caribou, the twin-turboprop DHC-5 Buffalo is a STOL utility transport. In the CAF it is also used in the search and rescue role, serving with 413, 424 and 442 Sqns. 424 Sqn aircraft 115463 is seen here at Greenham Common, a long way from its home base at Trenton, Ontario.
Operated by: CAF

Above: The CASA 212 Aviocar light utility STOL transport was designed primarily to replace the Spanish AF's mixed transport fleet of Ju52s, C-47s and CASA 207s but also to perform a variety of other military roles. In Spanish service it is used for passenger transport, paratrooping, cargo, medical evacuation, photographic survey, crew training and elec-

tronic intelligence work. The only other NATO operator is neighbouring Portugal. CASA 212A transport T12B-53/351-53 of 351 Escuadron was photographed at its home base of Getafe near Madrid in December 1985.
Operated by: Portuguese AF, Spanish AF

The West German military bought over 100 Dornier Do28 utility STOL aircraft. Each Luftwaffe wing was issued with at least three for liaison and light transport duties, while Marinefliegergeschwader 5 at Kiel received a total of 20. The latter aircraft were later fitted with a drop tank under each wing to extend their range. Displaying its new camouflage at RAF Fairford is 59+22 of MFG 5. **Operated by:** Federal German AF, Federal German Navy, Turkish Army

The Aeritalia G.222 twin-turboprop "mini-
Hercules" transport replaced the C-119 in
Italian Air Force service, and a navaid calib-
ration version is currently taking over from the
C-47 in this role. The G.222 is also one of two
main contenders in the contest to replace the
Dakota in Turkish service. MM62101 – a
G.222 of 311 Gruppo RSV, the Italian Air
Force trials and experimental unit – lands at
Greenham Common after a flight from its base
at Pratica di Mare. **Operated by:** Italian AF

Above: Recently introduced into RAF service is the TriStar K1, which equips 216 Sqn at Brize Norton. A total of nine ex-British Airways and Pan Am aircraft have been procured for use in the mixed tanker/passenger/cargo role, performed for the USAF by the KC-10. The TriStars were converted for tanking by Marshall of Cambridge, which fitted a refuelling probe above the cockpit and two hose drum units in the rear fuselage; in addition, refuelling pods will ultimately be carried under each wing. TriStar K1 ZD950 was photographed during a flypast at RAF Fairford in July 1985, when it was being used for flight trials. **Operated by:** RAF

Right: The McDonnell Douglas DC-10 wide-body trijet, known as the KC-10A in USAF service, bears a more than passing resemblence to the TriStar. But unlike the Lockheed type and the VC10, which can refuel at least two aircraft simultaneously, the KC-10 can accommodate only one at a time, using the boom/receptacle method. This limitation is however partly offset by a higher fuel flow rate. The KC-10, named Extender by the USAF, also has a drogue system installed near the boom to enable it to refuel USN/USMC and other probe-fitted aircraft. KC-10A 90434 of the 32nd Air Refuelling Squadron, 2nd Bombardment Wing, is seen landing at RAF Wittering. **Operated by:** USAF

66

The RAF has been successfully operating the VC10 C1 transport since the 1960s, so when surplus airline aircraft came on to the market it made sense to buy them up and convert them into tankers to meet the RAF's growing need for air-to-air refuelling. This work was carried out at BAe Filton, with standard VC10s being designated K2 and the Super VC10s K3. All have now been delivered to 101 Sqn at Brize Norton, where they operate alongside the VC10 C1s of 10 Sqn. VC10 K2 ZA143/D is seen here trailing all three hoses during a display at RAF Fairford. **Operated by:** RAF

A total of 808 Boeing C-135 Stratotankers were bought by the USAF for use in a variety of roles: tanker, cargo/passenger, airborne command post, and reconnaissance/ELINT. Some 792 of this total were KC-135 tankers, equipped with a flying boom which could also be fitted with a drogue to accommodate probe-fitted receivers. Some KC-135s are now being re-engined with JT3D (KC-135E) and CFM56 (KC-135R) turbofans. The CAF has five Boeing 707s designated CC-137, two of which can be equipped as tankers. KC-135A 80098 of the 906th ARS, 5th BW, from Minot, North Dakota, is pictured departing RAF Mildenhall. **Operated by:** CAF, French AF, Federal German AF (passenger only), USAF

The Nord 2501 Noratlas transport has been in service for over 30 years, and was operated in large numbers by the French and German air forces. The handful still in French service are now being replaced by second-series Transalls. Some ex-German aircraft remain in service with the Greek Air Force but are in urgent need of replacement. Photographed at Dubendorf is 123/312-BH of French Air Force training unit GI312, based at Salon. **Operated by:** French AF, Greek AF

The C-160 Transall twin-turboprop military transport was jointly developed and produced in France and Germany, principally to replace the Noratlas. After deliveries were completed the Luftwaffe found that it had more aircraft than it required, and a number were transferred to Turkey. The Transall production line has since been reopened to meet a French Air Force requirement. Some of the new aircraft are capable of in-flight refuelling, being equipped with a hose-and-drogue unit in the port undercarriage sponson. C-160D 50 + 81 of Lufttransportgeschwader 62, based at Wunstorf, is seen here at RAF Brawdy.
Operated by: French AF, Federal German AF, Turkish AF

The Handley Page Victor, with its subtly curved crescent wing and sinister but elegant nose section, is surely one of the most beautiful aircraft ever built. This converted bomber has been the mainstay of the RAF tanker force for many years, and proved invaluable in support of the ultra-long-range strikes carried out during the Falklands War. Sadly, the Victor's days must now be numbered as the VC10 and TriStar take over in the air-refuelling role. Seen here on take-off from RAF Scampton, bound for home at Marham, is Victor K2 XL189 of 57 Sqn. **Operated by:** RAF

The McDonnell Douglas DC-9 serves with the US forces under the designation C-9. The USAF uses this short-haul airliner primarily for aeromedical evacuation, dubbing it the C-9A Nightingale. Two C-9As operate in the passenger role, and three C-9C VIP aircraft are on charge with the 89th MAW. The US Navy employs the C-9B Skytrain II for passenger/cargo/logistics support, and the Marine Corps has two C-9s of its own. C-9A 10882 of the 435th Tactical Airlift Wing, based at Rhein-Main, lands at RAF Mildenhall just ahead of an inbound storm. **Operated by:** Italian AF, USAF, USN, USMC

73

Left: The Aérospatiale Alouette III utility helicopter entered large-scale employment with all three French services in 1970. The shipborne variant was probably one of the first helicopters to be fitted with a harpoon deck securing system designed to permit safe launches and recoveries in rough weather. The Alouette III can carry AS.11/12 wire-guided missiles, torpedoes, a tripod-mounted machine gun, and magnetic anomaly detection (MAD) gear in a towable streamlined container. French Air Force Alouette III 1265/AF was photographed while "patrolling" a nudist beach near Bordeaux! **Operated by:** Belgian Navy, French AF/Navy/Army, Royal Netherlands AF, Portuguese AF, Spanish AF, Greek Navy

Right: The extremely manoeuvrable Bolkow BO105 is in service with the West German Army in two versions, the BO105M utility/scout and the BO105P anti-tank helicopter. In the latter role it can carry HOT or TOW missiles. BO105M 80+54 of Panzerabwehrregiment 16, based at Celle, is pictured during its lively display at the last Fairford International Air Tattoo. **Operated by:** Federal German Army, Royal Netherlands AF, Spanish Army

Left: Development of the Boeing Vertol CH-47 Chinook transport helicopter began in 1956. Thirty years later it is still in production, for the US Army and RAF. As well as a large internal load, the CH-47D can carry three underslung items simultaneously. The characteristic noise of the Chinook's broad rotor blades has earned it the nickname "Wokka Wokka" amongst British Army troops. ZA675/FI, a Chinook HC1 of 240 Operational Conversion Unit at RAF Odiham, is seen landing at the Royal Navy Facility at Fleetlands. **Operated by:** CAF, Greek Army/AF, Italian Army, Spanish Army, RAF, US Army

Right: Another helicopter heavyweight is the Sikorsky H-53. In USAF service the "Super Jolly Green Giant" is used for rescue and recovery, and for tactical and special operations. The US Marine Corps version, known as the Sea Stallion, is used as a cargo/troop carrier and, like its US Navy counterpart, has a main rotor and tail pylon that can fold for stowage aboard ships. USN versions include vertical on-board delivery and minesweeping variants, and the current-production three-engined H-53E. Federal German Army CH-53G 84+25 of Heeresflieger Transportregiment 35, based at Niedermendig, was photographed at RAF Brawdy. **Operated by:** Federal German Army, USAF, USN, USMC

Above: The Westland Lynx has sold well within NATO, giving the alliance a healthy degree of standardisation in shipborne helicopters. The Naval Lynx can be armed with Sea Skua or Nord AS.12 missiles, depth charges and torpedoes, and can carry a lightweight dunking sonar to complement the Ferranti Seaspray radar. In Norway the Lynx is operated by 337 Skvadron on behalf of the Coast Guard. Against a background of gathering storm clouds, SH-14C Lynx 278 of 860 Sqn, Royal Netherlands Navy, prepares to land at Volkel. All Dutch Lynxes are shore-based at De Kooy, as indicated by the "K" on 278's fin. **Operated by:** Royal Danish AF, French Navy, Federal German Navy, Royal Netherlands Navy, Royal Norwegian AF, RN

Right: The British Army is the sole NATO operator of the land-based general-purpose/anti-tank Lynx, which is distinguished externally from the naval version by its skid undercarriage. An external pylon can be fitted on each side of the cabin to carry a variety of stores, including miniguns, rocket pods, and AS.11/HOT/TOW anti-tank missiles. Additional missiles can be carried in the spacious cabin for rearming in forward areas. Fitted with TOW missile launchers, Lynx AH1 XZ206 of Oakington-based 657 Sqn is seen en route to Salisbury Plain. **Operated by:** British Army

The Bell UH-1 Iroquois, popularly known as the "Huey," is probably the world's most readily recognised helicopter. Its sales total is unlikely ever to be surpassed by any other type, and it will almost certainly still be in service well into the next century. Late-build UH-1H 82-24045 of the HQ 1st Tactical Air Force of the Turkish Air Force was photographed at Eskisehir in November 1985. **Operated by:** CAF, Federal German AF/Army, Greek AF/ Army, Italian AF/Army/Navy, Norwegian AF, Spanish AF/Army, Turkish AF/Army, USAF, USN, USMC, US Army

The Aérospatiale Puma tactical helicopter was developed to meet a French Army requirement, and was also selected by the RAF. In the army support role the Puma has the virtues of speed and agility, but cannot stand up to the Size 9 army boot as well as the Wessex or Chinook. Photographed at RAF Brawdy, a long way from its home base at Montijo, is Puma 9505 of 751 Escuadron, Portuguese AF. Portuguese Pumas are also used for search and rescue. **Operated by:** French AF/Army, Portuguese AF, Spanish AF, RAF

The Sikorsky S-61 Sea King, US military designation H-3, first flew in 1959 and is still being licence-built by Westland and Agusta. The Sea King was designed as an anti-submarine helicopter, and the majority of current examples are employed in this role. Westland-built aircraft include search and rescue, commando and airborne early warning versions. Search and rescue Sea King Mk 41 069 (above) belongs to C Flight, 330 Skvadron, Norwegian AF, based at Oerland. Anti-submarine Sea King HAS5 ZA135/505 of 810 Sqn RN (right) arrives at Brawdy after a flight from its base at Culdrose. **Operated by:** Belgian AF, CAF, Royal Danish AF, Federal German Navy, Italian AF/Navy, Royal Norwegian AF, Spanish Navy, RAF, RN, USAF, USN, USMC

The Alpha Jet training and light attack air-craft, developed and built by the Dassault-Breguet/Dornier consortium, is powered by two SNECMA/Turboméca Larzac turbofans. Like most current advanced trainers, it has tandem rather than side-by-side seating. Weapons and stores, including an underbelly cannon pod, can be carried externally. Alpha Jet 40+35 of Jagdbombergeschwader 49, based at Furstenfeldbruck, lands at RAF Fairford. **Operated by:** Belgian AF, French AF, Federal German AF

The current glut of Western advanced jet training aircraft has made sales hard to find for some types. One successful contender in this crowded market is the CASA 101 Aviojet single-engined tandem trainer, which is now well established in the Spanish Air Force and has also been sold to two non-NATO air forces. Spain originally intended to use its Aviojets purely as trainers, but they are now being modified to carry external stores for offensive applications, even though the type is probably underpowered for such a role. Seen at RAF Mildenhall is E25-08/793-08 of 793 Escuadron, based at San Javier. **Operated by:** Spanish AF

Perhaps I am biased, but having flown about 25hr in the Hawk I consider it to be the best advanced jet trainer on the market today. The RAF also uses it in the weapons conversion role, and it can carry a ventral gun pod, bombs, rockets and, for air defence, Sidewinder missiles. This punchy little aircraft has an excellent rate of turn, and in air combat could make life very difficult for some of the more established and expensive fighters. Hawk T1 XX321 of No 1 Tactical Weapons Unit at Brawdy is seen here fitted with an Aden 30mm cannon. **Operated by:** RAF

The Fouga CM.170 Magister was for many years the French Air Force basic trainer. It is now being phased out slowly in favour of the Epsilon and Alpha Jet, although a number will remain in use for liaison duties. It was also replaced by the Alpha Jet in Belgium, though its low operating costs meant that a number remain in service at St Truiden. One of these aircraft is MT18, seen at Bruggen in the colours of the long disbanded *Diables Rouges* aerobatic team. **Operated by:** Belgian AF, French AF

Left: Aermacchi's MB.339 trainer/ground attack aircraft, designed to replace the MB.326 in Italian Air Force service, features the customary tandem seating and is powered by a single Rolls-Royce Viper. Like its rivals, the MB.339 can carry a range of external stores on wing pylons; it also has an internally mounted cannon in the nose. The MB.339 is the mount of the Italian *Frecce Tricolori* aerobatic team. Photographed landing at Greenham Common is MB.339A MM54493/37 of 212 Gruppo, based at Lecce. **Operated by:** Italian AF

Above: Siai-Marchetti SF.260M ST35 of 5 Sqn, Belgian AF, based at Goetsenhoven, was photographed while taxiing at Ramstein AFB. The SF.260 basic trainer is used by the Belgian and Italian air forces, and armed versions have been sold to a number of Third World countries. **Operated by:** Belgian AF, Italian AF

Above: The unusually shaped Rockwell T-2 Buckeye jet trainer was developed for the USN. It is fitted with an arrester hook to permit students to practice "live" carrier launches and recoveries. The T-2E, in use with the Greek AF, can be equipped with six wing hardpoints for external stores, and retains the arrester hook. Photographed at its Pensacola base is T-2C 157063/F31 of VT-10, Training Air Wing 6, USN. **Operated by:** Greek AF, USN

Right: What a success story the Lockheed T-33 is. This jet trainer has served with every NATO air force except the RAF, and is still in service throughout the world. Over 100 are still in USAF service, while in Canada over 60 are set to soldier on until 1995 at least. Having found its "T-Birds" cheap and easy to operate, the CAF sees no point in discarding them prematurely. CT-33A 133490 banks away from the camera over Ontario, its distinctive red and black rudder stripes identifying it as belonging to 414 Sqn. **Operated by:** CAF, French AF, Greek AF, Portuguese AF, Turkish AF, USAF

The USAF basic jet trainer since the mid-1950s, the Cessna T-37 "Tweety Bird" was due until recently to be replaced by the troubled Fairchild T-46. But now the new type's budgetary problems could well mean that refurbished T-37s will continue to serve for years to come. The Luftwaffe bought 47 T-37s with which to train its aircrews in the USA, where they are operated in the colours of the USAF. The USAF uses the OA-37 armed version for forward air controller work. This Turkish AF T-37B, seen at Eskisehir in November 1985, is 12804/TE-804 of 122 Filo, stationed at No 2 Jet Base, Cigli, near Izmir. **Operated by:** Federal German AF (USAF markings), Greek AF, Portuguese AF, Turkish AF, USAF

Over 1,000 Northrop T-38 Talon advanced jet trainers have been built, the majority for the USAF's Air Training Command though a few are in use at the US Naval Test Pilots School. A total of 46 were procured by the Luftwaffe and are operated alongside its T-37s at Shep-pard AFB, Texas. Photographed on the approach to its base at Monte Real is 2612, a T-38A of 103 Escuadron, Portuguese AF. **Operated by:** Federal German AF (USAF markings), Portuguese AF, Turkish AF, USAF, USN

Emerging as the clear leaders in the race for strike/advanced trainer orders are the Dassault-Breguet/Dornier Alpha Jet and BAe Hawk. Though Alpha Jet has a very healthy order book, Hawk protagonists see the British type as the ultimate winner. The Hawk's single engine gives only slightly less thrust than the twin Larzacs of Alpha Jet, and Hawk can also carry a larger payload further and faster. Although Alpha Jet entered development before Hawk, the latter was in service long before its rival, and when the Franco-German type did finally enter service it was some time before it was cleared for external stores. Illustrated are *(above)* Alpha Jet 41+60 of Jagdbombergeschwader 41 from Husum on the approach to RAF Linton-On-Ouse, and *(right)* Hawk T1A XX339 of 234 Sqn, 1 Tactical Weapons Unit, inverted over North Wales.

With their landing lights twinkling, F-104Gs 26+66 and 26+74 of Marinefliegergeschwader 2 taxi in at RAF Alconbury. The lights are now going out for the Starfighter, whose distinctive howl could once be heard all over Europe. Soon it will be confined to the air forces of Greece, Italy and Turkey. The last operates a large fleet of F-104s, including ex-Belgian, Dutch, German, Norwegian and Spanish aircraft. Italy and Turkey also operate the Aeritalia-built F-104S.